THE NEW GODS

WILLIAM O'DALY

WILLIAM O'DALY

THE NEW GODS

www.beltwayeditions.com

Printed in the United States of America 10 9 8 7 6 5 4 3 2 1

Cover Art: Zoe Norvell
Cover Image: "From Here, There" by Galen Garwood,
a painting from the "Meditations" series
Book Design: Jorge Ureta Sandoval
Author Photo: Courtesy of Kristine Iwersen O'Daly

ISBN: 978-1-957372-10-5

Beltway Editions (www.beltwayeditions.com)
4810 Mercury Drive
Rockville, MD, 20853
Indran Amirthanayagam: Publisher
Sara Cahill Marron: Publisher

TABLE OF CONTENTS

Foreword

Several years ago in an interview, the artist Galen Garwood asked William O'Daly whether the poet has always been an interlocutor between humanity and the divine. Garwood quoted from Wallace Stevens's Mount Holyoke lecture from 1951, "Two or Three Ideas":

> In an age of disbelief, or, what is the same thing, in a time that is largely humanistic, in one sense or another, it is for the poet to supply the satisfactions of belief, in his measure and in his style.

A poet, O'Daly answered, may be able to stand between humanity and what is godly, the things of God. A poem, then, might compose "an uncommon common language by which humanity and God or goodness, sublimity or beauty, might speak with one another." All art stands to play a similar role, among many different activities, making possible a communion between the mundane and the sacred.

But it is a communion which depends less on the words themselves than on how poets use them, on a poet's inner purpose and awareness, openness to what is revealed beyond the knowable, and insight into and humility before what is given them. A poet's participation in whatever forms of expression—those of art, say, or those found through the human body and its senses in the world, in all the elements of existence—helps transform experience into a language which constitutes a kind of prayer, petition, and way of giving.

Throughout *The New Gods*, the actual, concrete world—the world of rock, fire, rivers, rain, trees, blood, flowers, the whole earth—feels as filled with "intention as a stream might be to fill an ocean." A master translator of Pablo Neruda, with whom he has long shared certain sensibilities, scope, and breadth, O'Daly is a poet for whom prayer itself is corporeal, in the way, for example, sweat sours "elbows and clothes."

Each person's blood "salts its praise" for what love makes possible. It is the poet who "hammers distance into shape" and offers this to us in the form of poems. But the imagination, in a sense, is already there, outside, waiting in the things through which we find ourselves, ready to be built with our own "passion and wanting."

For we—all of humanity—"are the questions the stone and the river ask." If William O'Daly's poetry, like Neruda's or Lorca's, suggests an understanding of surrealism, it is akin to what has been said about Neruda's work, that it is closer in its humanity to Paul Éluard's, in this important way, than to André Breton's surrealist program. It is a surrealism of the vital world, of a language that marries "spirit and action" to a pure purpose, a sustained improvisation "between roots and sky" that binds the near with the far, distance with the here and now.

Like Neruda, O'Daly possesses an incarnational imagination that aspires to the infinite. His poems transfigure a Catholic conception, one without dogma or doctrine, into a vision abundant with new gods, not old. His poems find their morality in an ethics of the visible, the provocative reality of things in which, for example, "the burnt-out barn cants its shadow to the deep." In such a vision, hamburgers and a heap of fries matter as much, speak as incisively, profoundly even, as the vital moon.

"Wonder is enough," O'Daly writes, since it offers "the solace of not seeking." The poems in this book are as acutely attentive to elemental things as they are expansive. *The New Gods* is a poetry which burns with the fires of the acutely observed. Yet "in the hour's song" of each poem, one might "touch infinity, this small world."

As the poet Shaun Griffin wrote, "O'Daly, by choice, has taken the long road, Basho's road, to the interior. Something few choose these days."

Peter Weltner,
author of *Birds and Tree/In Place* and *Woods and the City*

THE NEW GODS

WILLIAM O'DALY

What is it the new gods seek—
children or destruction, combustion or love?
The mirror denies everything, possessed
of faith and the stories. Like amber
the dream is true. It will
keep us whole
when we leap in,
when we walk on or die out.

The Fire

. . . solvitur ambulando . . .

The rising sun spins a web of ferns,
red columbine, icy stream tumbling
from the cloud-hidden peak
through the sweltering canyon
to fill the ocean. Moss hangs from the madrone
like tails of the grazing horses
that'll rear up, step into a gallop
when the flutter of sparrows ignites.

Seven days hiking switchback passes,
bathing in glacial lakes, weary in muscles
and thought, we step from granite boulder
to granite boulder and into a wildflower meadow.
The body of summer rises from the grass of Parnassus
to touch with the intimacy of wings
the tangled limbs of the sky. Water splashes
over shallow stones, metal cups
jangle against the packs
and in our descent we climb
where the trail forks, washes out.
Scrabbling over scree and fallen pine,
we discover each other in the stream.

Dipping our cups, we, exhalations of God
live our full moment and later
as pigment, red clay in the mountain.
Days ago, our names began to read like trails
that never arrive, smelling of yarrow and smoke.
Our prayer is sweat souring creases, elbows, and clothes,
these trembling limbs and questions that abide in silence.

Farther on, we cool our feet in the stream
and for no reason I recall when,
in a hail of spitballs, a cloud of ennui,
our beleaguered teacher spelled it out—
in the event of an attack or an accident
at the reactor, and because we live in a state
of strategic importance, our hormones
could be separated from matter. Our brothers and sisters,
our friends, our dogs, our laughter
released as vapor.

The trail evaporates in gravelly sand.
The gulls squabble over a last scrap
of rotten clam. We pass under the highway
among stranded pools, slip the packs
from our backs, untie our boots. When
the dying wave soothes our aching feet,
excesses of light recede. In your hand
the knife joins dried fish and bread,
bread and wild onion. We are born,
a seed splits. Our blood salts its praise
for what we make possible tonight.

Driftwood flares, consumes our bodies
in a widening circle of light.
We tune our inner ears to the cries
of burning cities, two losses held hostage
on the stem. Could clasped hands preserve
the common world, we might break the charge
of death, hush the groans of the ebbing tide.
Listen . . . one drop, the next—the hissing of stones
as the rain begins to fall
in the unborn child's name.

We have no country to escape.
Our neighborhood lives on clearcut bluffs.
Every night we turn out the lamps
in a wave. They say when we enter
the violet gates of heaven, the body flames
in a marriage of spirit and action
so close to pure purpose
every word blossoms erotic.

Black rocks glint in the moon's tide—
a map of surrender unfurls.
It beguiles our sleeping eyes.
You and I, lost in darkness,
lie under separate stars
at the edge of firelight.

A Summer Prayer

With evening mist I perch on a blackened
and blasted boulder
at the confluence. The river's psalm incants
the flesh of the spirit, the dance
of the extinct. Dust of acorns
survives in bedrock holes
with the dying thunder,
with the first breath.

I plunge into a bitter pool
of the north fork,
my pulse quickens—a single thought
escapes like trout, like flecks of gold.
Blood departs the arms and legs
for the heart. Inner tides release
uncertainty to the extremities,
longing that flares out of reach.

The river choreographs how I change,
how I abide
when the current takes me.

I stroke hard toward the bank
and rise like an icy moon
along the forgotten path.

Christian's Animal

Every little thing wants to be loved.
~ Sue Monk Kidd

When you stare at me, do you see
yourself, eyes of porphyry?
Perhaps I could be your animal spirit
and roam the playa and the stars? Built
to last, ready to move on,
I climb the misty pinnacles of Guangxi.
Older than my age among the araucaria
of the lower Andes, I am patient
as ten thousand years waiting to see the canyons
of Coconino County, where surely
my memory will grow deeper.

I will be river or mountain, a galaxy
that moves according to gravity, to necessity,
to natural numbers and scent. Most days
I do my chores. But now I want to go
outside and wave to the seven dancing
children moving across the night.

I pray that one day they will return
and be what we no longer take
for granted.
A mourning dove enters a mineshaft
and I join hands with the lost, afraid of becoming
what I am not.
I kiss the darkness that knows I am not ready.
The more I love, the stronger I become.

Come Out of the House

They will say you are on the wrong road,
if it is your own.
~ Antonio Porchia

Before the house burns down,
open your eyes to the rain and the owl.
In the plaza a soldier is smoking—
the elm puts on new leaves.

My daddy doesn't want me to be
any artist, not even a rancher
like him. His sweat goes to deadbeats,
like the cattle and the songs.

I still have that part of me fire
transformed. Is it wrong
for a man to cry
at three in the afternoon?

Poet, don't you know
fire makes you young,
gives you something real
to fear?

In my pocket, I carry the jawbone of an ass.
I learn virtue
planting myself among the delphiniums.

Poet, feel the flames at your fleet—
feel this ground, like water in the earth.

Spring is demolishing the dead.
Wrapping myself in the sun's ribbons,
I am learning to be young, delirious
among the ruins at three in the afternoon.

Why do you keep fighting, poet
—sharing pain and joy in difficult times—
is it the ashes collecting on your teeth?

Why are so few born
at three in the afternoon? Why do I die?
Are words bitter seed or fierce anemone,
weapons or prayers?

Poet, what is your favorite color of kite?
Why are words never what they seem,
falling eyes, rising mouths, charging bulls, or smoke?

Will you remain on the earth
or flee like a lost river, an archaeologist chasing
the stars?

The Dream of Mount Liberty

Skeptical bell, fierce certainty of dust,
the snow-covered mountain
no longer hears its own ringing.
It knows no fear.
In its language
will does not exist.
Its rivers carry
the past in snow
that no longer falls.

Love in a Changing Climate

Touching your absent hand, I am like the saint
who wanders with the first yellow leaf,
the ease of what might be mistaken
for our familiar love. It's never easy
to sustain in the eyes what changes inside,
to feel the fear, the abandonment, and shame.
Listen . . . the wind is scattering our names. We are
the question the stone and the river ask.

Had I been with you when you died, I'd know
him who knows how to shepherd the dying home.
Illiterate birds ravel our lives with twelve strings
and we find love that takes the leap with us,
stays to clean up the birth of the cosmos,
the benevolent trees that burn like us.

The Story of Jacob

It came to pass, the young men cut down the trees
to feed the campfire and the cookstove,
to barter for wares or wives,
to carve arrows and bows, clubs and spears—
they built bonfires as gifts to the gods;
in later years they wearied of wandering
the desert of their own making, erected temples
and houses, corrals for horses and sheep.
The birds, having no place to preen
or nest or sing a lullaby, leapt
from the shores of Canaan
into the Mediterranean Sea—
forsaking life in Hebron and Shechem,
Dothan and Kadesh, they sought prophecies
of green pastures in the land of Ramses.
Holding fast to the sunlit waves,
they waggled their tails,
stilled their featherless wings
and rose from the floating world—tilting to catch the wind,
eluding the Man-of-War, the Great White.

Multiplying, they migrated among the reefs,
leapt to spy the umbrellas, the bikinis and hats
encrusting the beaches. They mastered evasion
and belief, took the hues of the rainbow
and renounced their bodies for ease;
settling in their ways, half formed,
they awaited conversion, longing for more. Angels,
they lived in a sexual era,
their dreams wrestling with silence—

the artichokes with their armor, the pharaoh
with his generosity toward those who want to die
in their own country. Who can blame
the exiled bird become a fish? Who can blame men
for their fascination with fire,
for seeking a bowl of soup
after a day plowing the borrowed field?
Stones are little more than flesh
when we bloom with the scant moon,
with ceaseless sowing or the grace
sequestered in the grape, in inimitable fear.

Who will be a talisman of forgiveness
and embrace faith simply as faith?
Wakening to the swallow's flight,
who'd rather kiss a fish than draw blood?
Rising to the inexhaustible light, we aspire.

Hestia

What you create—the bad? the good?—
creates you, sows the grace of song while you
tend the kettle—no time for the pantheon,
darkening blood, available light,
obsession, or uterus.

Pressed against glass, hand on hip, your hair
in a bun, the loose strands like wild roots
touch us, our open hands, our eyes, and once more
the soul. Our parallel lives spread like a bruise, like want, river or
barnacle or bread, the first time we speak
with the cloud like a moth burns in the sky.

Lightning comes from behind. The young
discover their nakedness, depart and do not stop—
the smile, the rancher, the slow dog, the horse tripped
with a rope, the artless loon, the blind judge—
together we dream alone, do not know or forget or cease,
or remember to let go.

Your body drips languor, you bleed and sweat
and endure what directs or murders us—time
and again, a woman imprisoned
by the gauze of selflessness.

One night, late, in the rain and in the doorway,
we might recognize this burning
as our own. We stand with you, Hestia.
Dreaming like a butterfly, may we choose
your transparent world?

Mysterious Figure

Is God a girl? you ask as we climb
the Coast Range, your taste for iron and salt
expanding beyond your 1,875th day.
Do numbers go forever? Our small car
rounds a curve
and catches sight of the shimmering sea.
If numbers keep going, there must be a day-itty.
You say it this way, your cheeks the color
of apricots, beautiful mind hungry as one bee—
no cloud, no chord, no stone,
no poem will ever be like yours. Today,
you blow on your alto saxophone
lonely numerals with love,
numbers that have no other.

I blow a kiss to the mystery
of who you are
as your fingers discover twilight.
Life moves with sweet intensity
when you blossom geometrically—
your lips touch infinity, this small world.

You play the wind, listen for the rain
and take flight with the ferocity of one drawn to song,
sculpting your own Greek isle.
With each breath you seek a heaven
that has no need of honey.

The Lives of the Children

The cloud is free only / to go with the wind. /
The rain is free / only in falling.
~ Wendell Berry

Born to lightning,
we reaped love and warp,
returned to the empty lot, to the advent
of democracy. We dug a fortress,
burrowed under an orange tree,
exposed the roots and inhaled the incense
of worm. Our lives hid among ghosts,
took shelter with dirty magazines
tied by a string and buried.

Pigeons scatter. Children flee
the cupola and their wings,
bearing *mea culpas* on their backs.
In street and meadow, mountain and tower,
they climb the ladder of heaven
never again to be warriors or angels.

One caught valley fever, another returned
to the womb and drowned,
others let go because
they'd had enough,
too much misery or bliss, others
were lost in the marshes of Vietnam,
or at the end of a defibrillated neighborhood.

Separate, apart, each of the other—
we are a single attraction,
a resistance, a theft,
a map of plunder in relief.

With the fullness of our arms,
we join the exiled and the wind.

Afraid to look, may we seek,
dark angel, the favor of your eyes?

The Unwritten Letter

Dearest K, in the afternoon I run a trail
through the forest, and enter a meadow
where the burnt-out barn
cants its shadow to the deep.
Flames, and the doors
hang by a hinge.
Frightened animals
flee into their lives
where the trail crumbles
at the bluff's edge—

Against the horizon
I look for you,
for a house by the sea,
for a life that opens
the rose in our blood.
K, do you listen for me
half passing in the wood
or see my eyes in the faces
of animals half in Paradise?

K, let me tell you
my coursing fear,
how some days
we live far from ourselves and
each other—so much farther, brushing
hundreds of miles like dust
from our clothes. I want to tell you
my blood sighs, but
I cannot open my fist.

You and I know
how it is simple
to make a pretense,
call it denial of the body
or soul's salvation, or a supple happiness
we shape with our hands.

Today, I send you the dusty rosehips
we picked in October's chill,
the memory of your fingertips,
the sun on your arms and blue scarf.
Earth offers us little time
to live in the harbor
the wound carves
between death and dream.

When we awaken
among the sparks
and shadows in our blood,
I fear everything
we must let go.

No kiss, no sky,
and the cold sun rolls
beyond the hidden mountain.

The Flag Is Burning

We, friend, are the body of the country
burning in the street,
eyes open against the sky,
the child running,
the mother on her knees
reaching for the soldier aiming,
the village on fire—the shrapnel littered ruins
of the hanging gardens
of Providence and Cheyenne,
snow falling over the blistered arroyo
in an ashen dance,
the stars surrendering white
over Pierre, the rain
penetrating the prairie,
the clothes and walls and pillows
spattered crimson,
the steeples congregating
in a phosphorus sky,
claiming God's bidding.
We are the tombs of brothers and uncles,
who send our sons and daughters into battle,
in the senate and the woodshed
our ties smoldering like oil slicks,
conviction flourishing like ivy
fueled by our breath,
we are the flag and the heart
from which it was sewn,
we are the dead who gather
burning in the child's mind,

the hunger that congregates
and cries out, *never again.*

To the Forty-Third President of the United States of America

Mr. President, our history speaks to us, the history of Chile
and China, El Salvador, Nicaragua, Somalia, Puerto Rico—
today, our solemn duty is to defy your willful aggression,
to parse provocative words and habits, your heroic battle
to distract us. Perhaps you think God will protect us
from the religious zealots who sanctify your rule,
from your opportunism and the race renewal,
the investiture you have assumed because, as
always, it is not yours. Let me ask
an obvious question.
                                        If we are to establish peace
and security for our nation, must we not do
everything in our power to end
the beginnings of war, must we not allow
our imaginations to craft a lasting peace?
Are not the children you would choose
to incinerate our own? We try on masks
to trick our isolated, frightened selves,
to propagate our sacred uncertainties
among the children of this blue planet,
a world we create and ruin every day.
                                                            Mr. President,
where can we walk, where may we sit down,
where will we work or rest, weep or pray,
what field does a man sunder and seed
in a country living only in memory, dying
every day at the hands of those who profess
to love her most? They say God loves America,

and that this *old bitch gone in the teeth* is
heaven on earth, in preemptive violence,
in obstinacy, in entitlements for the rich,
this murdered land, this, the people's
earth, is our reward for being right
no matter how wrong we are.
                                        What *urge and rage*
thrives in the American heart, that so many cheer
this obsessive, unilateral madness?
                                        Even through
precise layers of glass, the TV peddling
a thrilling efficiency, we cannot see them,
the ghosts that inhabit our malnourished
statistics, inhospitable closets, cold kitchens
where we eat meat and raise goblets of wine
to celebrate our belief that they are not like us.
I want to spend more time with my daughter,
my five-year-old, I want to see her, to know
she is alive. It is her *evening of the morning,*
she is just fine, though she implores me to tell her
the *acommitation of naked truth.*
                                        I imagine
Iraqis, weakened by sanctions, spending time
with their children. What do they play together,
what makes them laugh, what crude medicine
do parents spoon down fevered throats when
they too are roused from nightmares of fragile
necklaces of bone slung around the necks of
American fighters whose hearts we camouflage?
Who will witness the small charred bodies floating
in the Tigris, children writhing in pain, in smoking rubble,
in the ruins of Bab al-Wastani or the Mirjan Mosque,

severed limbs and glazed eyes that last night
followed their favorite stories by candlelight?
                                        Mr. President,
what does it mean when you say Saddam Hussein,
Butcher of Baghdad, official liar, terrorizes himself?
If he brings terror upon himself, will our dark angels
exterminate him or his already wounded people?
Would you answer Mr. Korb: *What if Kuwait grew carrots?*
What if Iraq's
major exports were fresh dates and cotton shawls
destined for white American women
longing for the exotic?
                              To be honest,
I've forgotten from what we must abstain,
yet we know how to prevent conception. *C'est la vie,*
you say, saddled up, ready to ride with your posse
across oil fields just like those in Texas.
It appears the one thing we cherish
more than petroleum or our children
is the greased machinery of destruction.

Afghanistan

Brokenhearted, shuddering land—
the shadows of tall palms melt
like the hands of children
in the blood dark dust.

Questions for Pablo

I.

Where did you leave it,
the poem not written?
The beginning, is it
a death or a birth?

II.

Does the rose kiss you
with its mouth full of blood?
Was it a smile or a wound
that devoured you?

III.

Unlikely sea, conflicted star,
do you still fear what you love?
Is it you who makes the gourds rattle
in my summer garden?
You who hammers
the distance into shapes?

The Turning Year

Raise your cup—
where last spring we perched on a boulder
still warm from all-day sun, and cast
our lines into the moonlit river.
Late thaw tumbled and whitened,
time slipped from the pools below.

Through grasslands and gorge,
you cleared a switchback trail
five hundred miles in my blood.
All summer, moist light spun
the leaves and purple clusters.
Then yellow mountain ash.

Now you sip wine
beneath the naked mimosa
and drift near sleep,
beyond flood-leveled plains
and the snowy mountains between us.

This casual moonlight
holds you, holds me,
where we are.
We share everything—
the deep red wine

of some distant summer
and the harvest moon
floating in our cups.

Hotel Fargo and the Gift of Long Island

Love's another departure.
~ Gwendolyn Brooks

We are gathered here, family and friends,
beside this nuptial river that flows forever
between the proud and peeling murals
of Gwendolyn's Mecca and the operatic stars
careening over Hell's Canyon and Manhattan.
While lightning sends rabbits scurrying
for their dens and horses thundering
through Central Park, we stand
among the infernal kingdoms of rippling wheat,
the steepled towers of profit and loss,
and celebrate this union
of heart and soul, joining ourselves and each other
where the patient groom waits
in his summer suit, perspiring in awe,
and the bride glides with perfect grace
from under the ancient banyan tree.
Keepers of the secret of changing light,
of the sustained improvisation between
roots and sky, islands and the sistine seas,
we pray that the steeping green leaves tell us
why lovers must stand always
on opposite sides of the rain,
casting a single shadow
across the sudden rim of the world.

Is it metaphysics or poppies
that make a marriage last?

And what do the white lilacs whisper
when we, more poor or richer,
curl in our bed like question marks?
Lying in the radiant meadow,
we greet the angels and together
learn the kiss of yes,
yes, everything I have is yours.

Four Moments

Map
Strands of web linger
in the branches, a bee stirs,
and the tangled shadows
promise a world without grief.

Bird

Every word, thicket, and stone
in this fractured stand of aspen—
living chord, sonata, a single cry—
settle the misty mountain peaks.

The Quiet Hills

Yellow moon rises
above the sugar pine
in the never-ending night—
ten thousand crickets.

Summer

Crows chase a raccoon
along the wooden fence—
into the silence of a sunlit yard.

To Fabulous Liars and the Truth

for Doug Jarman

From the first call to the cantina
in the Sonoran hills, your feet like fire
dance to Mack the Knife across the bar,
lighting the notes that migrate from down under
to the deepening sky, born and sung in this
season of wings. My friend, imagine, with our hands
with passion and wanting we built this life—
so right and today secret long-gone dreams of
shaggy-haired rockers, left under a sun that
blisters even the young. How can it be we've
known each other so long? Who knows
where we will be a hundred years
from today? No answer but laughter
singeing our hands and our feet,
our throats open to the falling stars.

Bears in Autumn

Whose eyes cool among the flames?
What is this hunger, the calm roiling the pond,
refusing to burn with the thicket
like the names of those forgotten?

They are excited, the young bears, heads emerging,
swimming with the white and blue currents of beginning—
they leave the forest, the cave of white light, no longer
underground.
Mama trudges because she must—protecting, helpless.
We stare at them, see what they want us to see—
could the Big Dipper be anything but a dipper?
But to the Romans it was Bear or Seven Plowing Oxen,
and now to the Europeans, Ursa of the Hour is a plow.

They say a trinity of bears still rules
over the earth. But can we be certain
they share one body—could it be ours?
We burn with the same conviction,
our faces open as we pick up the ax
and go about our father's business.

The Naturalist

...for my unborn daughter

1.

I've waited a long time,
little one, longer than a man
is supposed to, wandering
the diminished coast,
searching for extinct whales,
the migrating iris—some small, unclaimed breath
among the waves.
Will you come to feel
that all of this is for us,
that bringing you into our imagined world
was a selfish act?
Be patient my love.
Don't kick too hard
or drink your rage.
You are the long blue dawn
of every dying life.

2.

Little one, it is on clear, moonless
nights, driving the narrow road
between Red Wing and Plover,
I try to imagine the unseen you
floating silent, naked and blind,
in a paradise lost to the born.
When events, syllables, confusions and sadnesses
flutter in and out of my ears and mouth,
when they nest in my throat,

I want most to compose for you
the hour's song, a few brief lines
that will open your nursery window
to voices rising from the Mystic River,
to the current that carried you from a fiery amniotic lake
at the other end of the universe
and nudged you into this meteoric stream
crackling through our bodies,
into this glacial blood
shaping the fallen star.

The Chords

for Louis V. Johnson, in remembrance of Alex Johnson, 1988–2010

And so we go, hearts and minds
open on song—
coming home to the vital moon,
our fingers picking and falling across

each discovered chord,
rest and bridge, the little things
that confuse and steer us—
asynchronous oaks, chromatic evergreens
swaying beside a high mountain road
where we dream the sound
of the original key, Adam's calm acceptance
of his fate, Eve's once-perfect teeth. Beyond
the clouds, a silent hummingbird sails
on the icy currents of our grief.
Tomorrow lives underground
with no aim but to inspire a first breath.

Every day, chord by chord, may the dogs
of defeat forgive us, and when night settles
may we surrender to life, sip the compassion
of our brothers and our sisters,
and hold the most bittersweet kiss of our lover
a little longer before
the rain begins again.

Handout

Empty horns and the cautious hours begin
in uneasy absence
as fog gathers, thickens,
shielding a figure huddled,
a human shape. We pass a quilted arc
of frozen shoulders, hooded head fallen
like a dark petal in the corolla of night.
My pace quickens. My daughter, slowing
into her life, into the power of what she carries
in the fragrant bag swinging at her right hip,
stops. *Let's go…*, I say,
but she turns back as he looks up, his eyes
catching the dim lights of docked ships.
She hands him half a cheeseburger and a heap of fries—
he accepts and in my shame
I see how tonight he will eat. In the cold, clanging air,
the gulls compete for a few missed crumbs.

For Kawamura Yoichi

On the tenth anniversary of your death
the lavish bamboo drops a full moon
of yellow petals, little tongues
singing the ancient songs
to whoever will listen—
the nighthawk gives all he has,
opening his eyes among the stars,
Buddha sits with angels beside the wild river
and laughs, touching mountain and cloud,
and a new generation waits to blossom
with the green rain of distant samsara.

Hug Point

I.

Tonight in this rented cabin
above a last gasp of creek
and the hereafter of ocean—
the day lives, choreography
of gulls and light, ever changing,
wave roaring on dark wave,
continual, necessary. I want to be
for you a rock anchored in sand,
the current you will never chart.
Your tidal heart speaks the dialect
of indecipherable birds, a song
I go on learning. Teach me
the spirit world, teach me
the language of love.

II.

Wave on wave tumbles to the cliff—
the sea returns, creating itself
in the secret beating of the heart
against silence. The cliffs are abandon,
the waves a kind of time, a whisper
we hear too clearly, without rest.
The rumbling is hunger, buried
intimacy, and silence my mute
want of you. Beyond the waves
we watch who we are together,
our blue love a migrating whale
rising in song, descending in the light

we've come to know only
in our passing, we who are
so difficult to decipher
when we pray, passing
hand in hand
into immensity.

Bird Experiencing Light

We see by means of something that illumines us;
which we do not see.
~ Antonio Porchia

When the ocean breathes,
when light collects and
violets emerge drenched
from broken fields, you are born.

Alive by the hands of surgeons
your mother smiles. Helpless,
I stand in the operating room,
no longer able to feel afraid

as the nurse lays you in my arms
and you, little bird of the spirit, perch
on this burning branch
with a single cry.

Someday, angel of the seashore, you will ask
and I will tell—but now
I beg you, take your place
among the fragrant names,

the *Ciara* of forgetting, metal or leaf,
incandescent wind or knowing
when fossils ring in the buttes,
in deepest faults, in the lost library.

Soon enough I'll merge onto the freeway, stay far
to the right, ever so slow. Safely home
we'll swaddle you, and there we'll be,
our transparent lives and your wings.

Wonder is enough. Our bodies will
say it is so, even as the ebullient flowers
greet you forever, and then
with the colors of our tears.

Origin

Long ago you and I struggled to be born
among the standing stones,
underground fire, mineral rain,
furrows of imagination yellowed by the sun.
Our immobile blood burned blue
even as the wind shaped
our serene incarnation. We deciphered
the doors of the earth, found the one to open
on who we would become.
Our still-closed eyes strived to name oneness,
to behold the mystery of our bodies
falling in a rage of flame, in the rhythms
and textures of our appetites. We tuned ourselves
to sow and reap, shepherd and slaughter,
to be true to many selves
and the singularity
from which we came.
Forging weapons that turn night to day
we meditated on the clouds
littered with the psalms of migrating birds.
We mourned the wild horses,
the range stripped of native forage.
The prayer wheel spun us at our core
as we labored to learn that how
we live is what we leave behind.

Returning to the solace of not seeking,
we need no face or syllable or seed,
as we come to know in our hearts
what we cannot know any other way.

Tonight…

Staring up through the roots of the sky
I see all things arrive
from above and below,
each born to the other
and free of their bodies—
the light of yellow leaves,
the nebula of the inner eye.

Tonight I come from water and salt,
from what binds us together
and what pulls us apart,
to offer my empty hands,
my solitude and its wings—
the touch, our cyclic motion,
the indelible beauty of a dying star.

Tonight, lost to truth, not able to know
or name it, I hold close the silence
at the core. The imploding points
of light that brighten our eyes
turn our suffering into spirit—
our fear into water, grief into air,
confusion into earth, ignorance into fire.

Tonight the chords arrive from the darkness
between stars, and the pulsing light
of an inconceivable harmony
spins a requiem for our lips,
for the cadence of our tears—
the cosmos, the scheme of things
in which every leaf is a watershed.

Tonight I settle in the radiant dust
of memory, the slender
breath of bodies entwined
in bel canto for an eon or an hour—
when sudden lunacy blooms in laughter—
in that gravity, in the electrolysis of love
the streaming seed stalk of the visible.

Tonight I once more climb the ladder
of heaven with my flesh and my robe,
taste what it is to possess nothing
and owe everything to the tides
and the stars—the voice clear
as the voice of the mourning dove.

Afterlife

Seven petals, seven seas,
seven words like moths
wet with night—
we share everything.

Obscured by the living rain,
leaves gather what we make
of the yellow bells at dawn—
the horizon rings us
plural again.

Seven clouds oblivious
to seven cathedrals of the sun—
we strike an accord,
you and me, with the scent
of orchid, shattered beauty
discovered in nearby nebulae.
We ravel, every day ringing
in seven songs
without names.

For Neruda

Ride your pale horse
through the meadow tonight
among the black skirts of the sky—
bring into your hands the exiled light,
the litanies of broken glass and bone…

We will hide you in the flower garden,
in the closet when the police close in.
You will lie under a blanket in the back seat
of the sedan headed south, and later climb
into the Andes, your typewriter stuffed
in a saddle bag. As your exposed heart opens
to the waterfall, to the river
of shattered hands, your two vaquero guides
will roll their eyes. On reaching the pass you will
barely notice the goats perched above, staring
at you—stripped down to the man you are,
you no longer search for your scars,
your country, artifacts, women,
the daughter who died in the house of flowers,
the brother buried at night, where farmers
still dig for water.

Pablo, tie your horse to the night,
sit with me in the lost city on a patio
ringed by geraniums and quiet hills,
before the dawn arrests our sense of beauty—
in an hour the river will run
with the color of blood…

You will listen for green rain
falling through the dense kilometers,
speak to snow in the mountains,
discover gratitude in fields where women search
for a shard of bone, the back of a skull
empty as a womb,
a foot still in its shoe—
the youngest son, preserved in the dry earth
where politicians hide their silences,
their words, their money belts,
gunpowder and disease.

Let me pour you sparkling wine
stirred with the juice of pomegranates,
offer handfuls of mountain blueberries,
a ladle brimming with olive oil
to drizzle over onion and tomato,
on crusty bread—then a poem of friendship,
some woolen socks, the bonfire and a guitar.

Ride your weary horse
from the assaulted coast, rest
on beds of Mexican salvia, African daisies,
delphiniums, where the Greek gods wrote
love letters to the creatures
who save us from ourselves…

What can we say to the ruined star?
Brother of my breath, how can we sing,
any of us, how will we remember to live
for nothing, how are we to laugh as we scatter
petals over your ashes? I never saw you cry but
do my best to let your words weep,

to play simply, to flow like the blood
of the children, to sweat
the gifts of the body and presume the soul.

Ride your horse where the dead
and the living
rise from their graves.
Witness the tombs opening,
the vertical stones falling, the guiding eye
colliding with vision and belief…

Around us
in churches and mosques, the innocent are falling,
praying lavishly and alone. The river
that carries us succumbs to concrete and steel:
the words you shouted for beautiful Victor
on your death bed, the taunts as he died
at the hands of the torturers—
words so brutal, so ugly
they take the breath away.

Thousands are leaving their apartments
and entering La Avenida de la Paz
lined by Chile's own *Guardia Civil*,
machine guns and batons but no one
gives a damn, thousands join the procession
to the General Cemetery, scattering flowers
over your casket. An eagle glides and tilts
toward the coast, heading perhaps
for an empty nest. We all
have arrived, the living and the dead
shouting, *Pablo Neruda, presente!*

Return to Isla Negra. Matilde will warm a meal—
in the splendor empty bottles and poems
like roots will wash up on the shore,
returning all you have given.

Conspire with me among the hills,
the black oak and the vines.
Let me plant a kiss of salt
on your forehead. Let us free ourselves
and with a single throat praise the summer grass,
keep time with the dancer who flares
in the first dark hour before the Perseids streak
across the emptiness.

The Dreamers

I.

One night a boy emerges from among the clothes
hanging in the open closet and stands beside the bed.
He is dressed in dark woolen trousers and a white shirt
buttoned at the neck, and his shiny black hair is slicked
back, as they wore it in his day. He slowly reaches out to me—
in his hand a glass of water, iridescent—
the colors are my voice, an offering drawn
from the mineral spring
of the first beginning.

II.

Now I stand at his grave, where the world ends
in the cormorant's cry, and I can hear
the horse's tail swishing among the trees.
Like secret phosphorus, a gift of woolen socks
binds the weaving hands to oceanic light.
The plutonic rocks born of the far south
rise from the shelves into our consciousness,
bearing the volcanic words he left to us.
His wild-haired love still sings as she dusts
the weeping figurehead, the small black god,
and the brass telescope, a gift from the French,
and watches for his return from mountain or sea,
where side by side they live on
like water or inevitability.

The Dream of the Waterfall

The old stones stream in the arteries
of the gods, and every moment the river
changes, our bodies change, love changes
everything and we will never be the same.
The river empties into the burning field,
collides in light and shadow,
where in the caves of forgotten animals
the prehistoric dream is in motion.
It flows on in darkness. It does not stop.

In Franconia Gorge

Is this ever-descending water
human tears? Do they mean nothing?

Will the stone heads that weep
in the late afternoon fade away?

Without you, how will we weep
when we need to?

How will the earth smell
after the last drops of rain?

Steering the Gyre

for Will Emery

You and I are invited, we are here,
gathered and silent; Rexroth's voice thrills
magnificent in our throats. He fills the living room
like a leopard or a rope—unseen he frees
himself: *I write poetry to seduce women and*
overthrow the capitalist system, in that order.
He laughs. Everyone has a history of revision.
Even Voltaire, with his particular flair,
tutored the young in the physics of love
and frightened the Church. After Lorca
was executed at Fuente Grande, blood ran
in the streets. Don Pablo's awestruck and furious
flowers repeated themselves to the waves,
the house opened to the clanging bells,
to those who mourned, but I cannot
touch his blood, or *his* blood. It runs
on the moon. The ocean fills, the flame gasps
in the trenches, dies again and writes
itself in the sands of the Algarve.

Pharmacopoeias nestle, shady oaks
caw endlessly, and I waste my life
where the bloodied sea cannot touch me.
In search of Lola Montez, petal of
forgetfulness, I switch back
into the Sierra, past the three lakes
of Loch Leven. Mount Judah overlooks
my glacial night, waves of granite breaking
where memory and snow are never enough.

Only Mount Lassen gives distance meaning, farther
than I can see, crossing creek and scree and
black volcanic rock until my feet ache and ink flows.
I nearly died there. And you—you sail
with family, friends, a pilot you trust
who places his faith in the veteran stars—
guiding the Gyre from Halifax, past
Betty's lighthouse dreaming on its island,
past the Bay of Fundy and the brackish waters
of Bras d'Or to the livid hibiscus of
Bermuda, where now you may be strumming
from the bottom of your well,
a lost horizon shining there,
the leeward leaning sea
attenuating the waves, full
of the wind's voltage in motion.

Solitary time, misshapen stone
that arrives too late—
the Buddha sits or runs in place
under the Bodhi tree, in this gold rush town
between Newcastle and Cool, despite
what the homepage says not any kind of Eden,
a thousand feet above Marysville
where Sun Yat-sen composed the Chinese constitution,
south of Peking and Paradise, California,
almost the same place.

All summer, the furniture writes poetry.
Horses whinny, opine in their sugar-
pine meadow, where the ghost train passes high
above the American River Canyon,
where nights and days are the same

as these, only more florid. Words
coalesce, roost in nested boxes,
syllables hide under small blue veils
among the clothes and the emperors
who betray their infamous season. I arrive
nowhere, like Seferis's heroes,
in the dark. Hope chains me
to the rock. Disappointment enthralls.
I recite *el poeta del pueblo*
in public, under a thousand absent stars.
I say the words to release the rivers
that cradle this valley, to find solace
on your churning sea. Where you sail,
can you feel the night leap and
distant volcanoes congregate—can you hear
the exaltations of gnats
praising the light?

The Eastern Sea

Like you, I have sought
the fate of the wave,
the burnt mast, the water birds
gliding near as a prayer. And so
as the eastern sea passes
its ring of opal light to the sky,
I promise I will pass the ring
of the sea to my daughter.

Always, the mermaid speaks of love.
The beggar cries that his sandals
were stolen by Jesus. My daughter
asks me to hold those fragile rings,
to hold the sea that breaks with gravity's secret
and washes over our cold bare feet
until she has a song to sing to it.

Heron Dances Over the World

Even you're not watching
as you spread your black tattered wings
and step among the colors of the physical world—
spindly legs conjure the symbol for infinity
in red earth, in fresh blue snow and white mist.

Endangered islands bloom, the wetland fills
with mountain shadow. In a parallel universe
your reflection moves to its inner calling,
to folded granite, music of the waterfall.

You live as hidden origami, with creases
and abandon, intricate patterns that resist
the receding shore. You circle, an equation
neither eyes nor lips can touch—motion that can't be solved
or written on the tongue. You do not stop to preen
among the battered dunes.

Your cry wrings iron from irony,
recalls the silent bells, laments the love
I've forgotten. You breathe closer to the swaying aspen
than to the orphaned moon and the tide's pull.
In this dance you create, like a beetle,
your own being.

The Woodcutter

Shuddering when eyelids touch
the spirit of incandescent stone,
wind of the red violin—by these
we steer the little fishing boat
beyond the horizon, sipping
unearthly cocktails rimmed in the salt
of an undiscovered sea.

In summer we sit on the beach,
and in winter crowd the hearth's mosaic.
Waves in the gardens of love grow well here
as do ceaseless fire and Andean snow.
With hurricane lovers' lips, we kiss
Chile, carry the conversation
like grains of rice. We laugh
like they laugh.

Flying in debt
across the ridiculous abyss,
we live by the tenderness
of slaughtered sheep and *los desaparecidos.*
Crackling. Silent.
The barmaid and the poet make love
on the threshing floor of Chillán
while we dine on *camarones*
and the woodcutter sharpens his ax.

For My Wife

Let us lie naked in the shade,
let the breeze
caress us.

As the sun descends—
a kiss of honey
on intimate lips.

Solace

The rising moon
holds the light
of a windblown star.

I spit out the bone.
All that remains
is the sacred.

The Ruins

In words, neither cloud nor dream can exist—
even the olive tree, silvery
in winter, turns slate blue, and the light
of an extinguished star
empties the sky.

Navigating by the rose, we steer
without pause through burning ruins.
Children swarm among the old ones struggling
up the stone steps to South Heaven Gate.
You're not old, the trains are old,

and from here, you can see the songs too
are ancient. I'm not partial
to romantic love, to politics or speeches,
and even if a god designed
the cathedral and the shark,
we like the wave
eventually will empty—
shall we give the earth back to our feet?

NOTES

"A Summer Prayer": The site of this poem is the confluence of the north and middle forks of the American River near Auburn, California. That foothill region, known as "Gold Country" since the Gold Rush in 1848, have been home to Nisenan, Maidu, and Miwok peoples for millennia.

"Bears in Autumn": Based on "Transition," a painting by P. Findleton from the exhibit "Animal House: It's a Zoo Out There," Sacramento Fine Arts Center, Carmichael, CA, February–March 2013.

"Christian's Animal": Based on "Christian's Animal 1," a painting by Christian Sahota from the exhibit "Animal House: It's a Zoo Out There," Sacramento Fine Arts Center, Carmichael, CA, February–March, 2014. The epigraph is from *The Secret Life of Bees*, by Sue Monk Kidd, Viking, 2002.

"Come Out of the House": The epigraph is from *Voices*, by Antonio Porchia, translated by W.S. Merwin, Copper Canyon Press, 2003.

"Heron Dances Over the World": Based on "Got to Dance," a painting by Gary Edward Foster from the exhibit "Animal House: It's a Zoo Out There", Sacramento Fine Arts Center, Carmichael, CA, February-March, 2014.

"Hestia": This poem originated based on a painting of the same title by the artist Stephen Linstead. The ultimate shape of its voice and imagery came in response to a painting by Cheri Guerrette, "Not Participating".

"Hotel Fargo and the Gift of Long Island": This epithalamion was written for Benjamin and Lynne Curry and was read by the poet at their wedding on July 20, 1996. The epigraph is from "The Blackstone Rangers," by Gwendolyn Brooks, *Blacks*, Third World Press, 1994.

"Love in a Changing Climate": Loosely based on the poem "The Illiterate," by William Meredith. Original draft written in a workshop conducted by Patrick Donnelly, based on Meredith's poem, New Hampshire Poetry Festival, 2019.

"Origin": Based on "The Mountains Melting," a painting by Ann Ragland Bowns, Bold Ex Art Exhibit, Sacramento Fine Arts Center, Carmichael, CA, September 2019.

"The Eastern Sea": In memory of Denise Levertov and Gray Foster who, as a tenderhearted consequence of the friendship they developed late in their lives, passed on an unforgettable gift to my family.

"The Fire": The epigraph, *solvitur ambulando*, is a Latin axiom literally translated as "it is solved by walking." Most often attributed to Saint Augustine, the phrase was said to be spoken by Diogenes of Sinope when he replied to Zeno's paradoxes on the unreality of motion by standing up and walking away.

"The Lives of the Children": The epigraph is from "The Law that Marries All Things," by Wendell Berry, T*he Selected Poems of Wendell Berry*, Counterpoint, 1998.

"The Story of Jacob": Based on "Ode to Jacob," a painting by Alexandra M. Ulloa from the exhibit "Animal House It's a Zoo Out There," Sacramento Fine Arts Center, Carmichael, CA, February–March 2013. The line "would rather kiss a fish than draw blood" is a response to a similar phrase in Sam

Hamill's poem "A Lover's Quarrel", *Destination Zero*, White Pine Press, 1995.

"To the Forty-Third President of the United States of America": Written in 2003 for the "Poets Against the War" organization founded by Sam Hamill. First read publicly at "A Poetry Reading to Honor the Right of Protest as a Patriotic and Historical American Tradition," which took place at First Congregational Church of Manchester, VT, on February 16, 2003. Direct or paraphrased quotations included in the poem range from Ezra Pound, Anne Frank, Kyra Gray O'Daly, Lawrence Korb, and George W. Bush.

"Tonight…": Based on "Twilight Nebula," a painting by Linda Heath Clark from the exhibit at the Sacramento Fine Arts Center, Carmichael, CA, September 2019. The phrase "electrolysis of love" is from Kenneth Rexroth's poem "The Signature of All Things," *The Complete Poems of Kenneth Rexroth*, Copper Canyon Press, 2003. I also thank Elaine Pagels for her scholarly musings on Gnosticism and my colleague, Lewis Moeller, for passing along watershed wisdom.

"The Ruins": South Heaven Gate is symbolic of Taishan, or Mount Tai, the most venerated of China's five sacred mountains. For 2,000 years, Taishan was the place where the emperor paid homage to Heaven and Earth; its many masterful artworks exist in perfect harmony with the natural landscape.

ACKNOWLEDGMENTS

Many thanks to the publishers, journals, and other media in which the poems listed here were first published, often in earlier versions.

"A Summer Prayer": *Mouse Eggs*, Autumnal Equinox issue, September 2021; Montreal, Canada, print and online.

"Afterlife": *Terrain.org*, 2022, online.

"Bears in Autumn": *Tiferet: Fostering Peace through Literature and Art*, Fall 2016, print and online. *Paws Healing the Earth* (anthology), River Paw Press, 2021.

"Bird Experiencing Light": *Abrazos & Letters from the Self to the World*, DoveTails 10th Anniversary Anthology, a publication of Writing for Peace, 2021, print.

"Christian's Animal": *Life and Legends*, Inaugural Issue, Summer 2014, print and online.

"Come Out of the House": *Mouse Eggs*, Autumnal Equinox issue, September 2021; Montreal, Canada, print and online.

"For Kawamura Yoichi": *Sacramento News and Review*, September 2, 2010, print and online.

"For Neruda": *The Road to Isla Negra*, chapbook of poems, Folded Word Press, 2015.

"Four Moments": *Yarrow and Smoke*, chapbook of poems, Folded Word Press, 2018.

"Handout": *Clover*, Vol. 4, December 2012, print; P*erspectives on Arts*, Summer 2013, print.

"Heron Dances Over the World": *Life and Legends*, Inaugural Issue, Summer 2014; *Sacramento Voices* (anthology), Cold River Press, 2014. *Yarrow and Smoke*, chapbook of poems, Folded Word Press, 2018. *Paws Healing the Earth* (anthology), River Paw Press, 2021.

"Hestia": *Tiferet: Fostering Peace through Literature and Art*, April 2014, print and online.

"Hotel Fargo and the Gift of Long Island": *CutBank*, Vol. 72|73, June 2010, print.

"Hug Point": *Stanislaus Connections: A Gathering of Voices*, online, November 2006; *Sacramento Voices*, Cold River Press (anthology), 2014; *MAENAM: Of Water, Of Light* (anthology of poems and photographs), Marrowstone Press, 2014.

"In Franconia Gorge": Published as "Questions for Franconia" in *Water Ways*, chapbook of poems, with prose and photographs by J.S. Graustein, Folded Word Press, 2017; "Waiting for the Big Bang: Voices and Visions," Galen Garwood (artist), online, 2021.

"Love in a Changing Climate": *Abrazos & Letters from the Self to the World*, DoveTails 10th Anniversary Anthology, a publication of Writing for Peace, 2021, print.

"Mysterious Figure": *CutBank*, Vol. 72|73, June 2010, print.

"Origin": *Terrain.org*, 2022, online.

"Questions for Pablo": *The Road to Isla Negra*, chapbook of poems, Folded Word Press, 2015.

"Solace": *Medusa's Kitchen*, January 14, 2011 (under the title "Monday"); *Yarrow and Smoke* (under the title "Monday"), chapbook of poems, Folded Word Press, 2018.

"Steering the Gyre": *Narrative*, Spring 2009, print and online.

"The Chords": *Clover*, Vol. 4, December 2012, print.

"The Dream of Mount Liberty": *Waterways*, chapbook of poems, with prose and photographs by J.S. Graustein, Folded Word Press, 2017.

"The Dream of the Waterfall": *deLuge*, Summer 2016; *Waterways*, chapbook of poems, with prose and photographs by J.S. Graustein, Folded Word Press, 2017.

"The Dreamers": *The Road to Isla Negra*, chapbook of poems, Folded Word Press, 2015; "Waiting for the Big Bang: Voices and Visions," Galen Garwood (artist), online, 2021.

"The Eastern Sea": *Waterways*, chapbook of poems, with prose and photographs by J.S. Graustein, Folded Word Press, 2017.

"The Fire": *Yarrow and Smoke*, chapbook of poems by William O'Daly, Folded Word Press, 2018.

"The Flag Is Burning": *OccuPoetry*, Issue 4, October 2014, online.

"The Lives of the Children": *Mouse Eggs*, Autumnal Equinox issue, September 2021; Montreal, Canada, print and online.

"The Naturalist": *Great River Review*, 1998; *The Poet's Child* (anthology), Copper Canyon Press, 2002.

"The Ruins": *RATTLE*, Issue 34, Winter 2010, print (former title: "To the Antiphonist"); *Yarrow and Smoke*, chapbook of poems, Folded Word Press, 2018.

"The Story of Jacob": *Tiferet: Fostering Peace through Literature and Art*, Summer 2014, print and online.

"The Turning Year": *ColoradoBoulevard.net*, "Mapping the Artist," posted with an interview with William O'Daly, conducted by Kathabela Wilson, April 9, 2016, online.

"The Unwritten Letter": *Tiferet: Fostering Peace through Literature and Art*, Issue XV, 2010.

"The Woodcutter": *The Road to Isla Negra*, chapbook of poems, Folded Word Press, 2015.

"To Fabulous Liars and the Truth": *Yarrow and Smoke*, chapbook of poems, Folded Word Press, 2018; *Abrazos & Letters from the Self to the World*, DoveTails 10th Anniversary Anthology, a publication of Writing for Peace, 2021, print.

"To the Forty-Third President of the United States of America": "Poets Against the War" website, 2003; *Cry Out: Poets Protest the War* (anthology), George Braziller, Inc., 2003.

The New Gods and I have received the generous assistance and encouragement of many bright spirits and voices, the abiding friendships and inspiration of more individuals than I can list here. I hope you know who you are and the depth of my appreciation.

For editorial suggestions and support my gratitude to Bob Herz and Stephen Kuusisto of Nine Mile, Elaina Ellis, and Rose Auslander. My longtime friend and fellow founder of Copper Canyon Press, the late Sam Hamill, benefited the work with his belief, shared values, and activism. Folded Word Press published three of my chapbooks, Editor-in-Chief J.S. Graustein collaborating on the second, all of which helped engender this volume. Galen Garwood has lent his publishing skills, friendship and collaborative energies, and exquisite images throughout the years. A deep bow to mentors Kenneth Rexroth, Philip Levine, and James J. McAuley.

Kristine Iwersen O'Daly's editorial counsel, faith, and cheer helped keep the flame burning for this book, even as I fulfilled translation and other commitments over many years. Our daughter Kyra inspired again and again, without intention but with her observations and way of being in the world. Milton Rowland, Will Emery, Louis Valentine Johnson, Sam Green, Lois P. Jones, Juniper Moon, Zachary Marcus, Kathryn Hunt, and Patti Pattee have graced the work with generosity and insight.

My mother and father, brother and sister, and the whole clan have nourished the work with their love and support.

My endless gratitude to Indran Amirthanayagam and Sara Cahill Marron of Beltway Editions for bringing *The New Gods* into the world.

Beltway
EDITIONS
THE NEW GODS
PRINTING WAS COMPLETED
IN SEPTEMBER 2022 FOR BELTWAY EDITIONS